WHAT DO WE MEAN BY 'GOD'?

A little book of guidance

KEITH WARD

First published in Great Britain in 2015

Society for Promoting Christian Knowledge
36 Causton Street
London SW1P 4ST
www.spckpublishing.co.uk

British Library Cataloguing-in-Publication Data
A catalogue record for this book is available from the British Library

ISBN 978–0–281–07328–3
eBook ISBN 978–0–281–07329–0

Typeset by Graphicraft Limited, Hong Kong
First printed in China
Subsequently digitally printed in Great Britain

eBook by Graphicraft Limited, Hong Kong

Contents

1

Who or what is 'God'?

For many people today believing in God is really quite difficult. There are lots of ideas of God around which people find distasteful or unacceptable. For example, two of the best known paintings in the Western world portray God in ways that, unfortunately, give rise to quite false ideas of who, or what, God is. One is Michelangelo's painting of the creation of Adam, on the ceiling of the Sistine Chapel in Rome. In that painting, God is shown as a very well-developed, well-muscled specimen of humanity with long white hair and a flowing beard. He is just like Adam but a little older and with a bigger beard. This sort of representation of God in art was, of course, quite unknown in ancient Jewish tradition, which expressly forbade the making of any images or pictures of God at all. In Islam, too, no pictures are allowed in mosques, which is why such beautiful techniques of writing in decorative Arabic script evolved in that tradition. It might well be held that Michelangelo, for all his genius, broke that ancient prohibition on picturing God, and subsequent Western thought has paid the price.

Another well-known picture of God creating the universe is seen in 'The Ancient of Days', by William Blake.

Again, God is a well-muscled human being with a flowing beard and long white hair. In his hand he holds a pair of compasses, with which he is measuring out the world. When Blake drew this picture, he was in fact portraying the sort of God that he thought was a bad God, an interfering measuring God who squashed and repressed the human imagination. For Blake, this was a sort of anti-God. Unfortunately, most people do not realize that, and they take Blake's picture to be a depiction of God as he really is.

These paintings have had an unfortunate effect, because they are such good paintings and because the power of visual imagery is so strong that we find it hard to get out of our minds the idea of God as a man with a long flowing beard sitting just above the clouds or in the sky. We can get more sophisticated, and say, 'Well, I know that there is no actual physical form in the sky. We have been up there in space-ships and satellites, and we know there isn't anything there. And I know that he isn't just a little bit further away either, just beyond Alpha Centauri. No, God is not physical at all. He is a purely spiritual being.' But even if we try to get sophisticated, we might still think of God as a particular being: a purely mental being, who thinks in much the same way as we do, one thing after another; who decides, in much the same way as we do; who makes up his mind whether to do this or that, and perhaps changes it at a later date; and who feels in much the same way that we do, so that he feels sad when we do something wrong and happy when we do something good (which must mean he's depressed most of the time). In general, he has pretty well human feelings.

So God is seen as very much like an invisible human being, an immortal one; like the old Greek gods, he is human in character but immortal and invisible. This God is still a mind, rather like ours though better; he is out there somewhere; he is apart from us. He is perhaps just beyond the edge of the universe; he is a separate being. So we say that God is transcendent; he transcends everything in the physical universe. But he is, nevertheless, another mind.

But this is just as false a picture of God as is Blake's or Michelangelo's. It is quite essential, when we start thinking about God, to put this picture out of our minds completely. Whatever God is, he has never, in the orthodox Christian tradition, been thought to be a finite mind, even if very wise and powerful, somewhere in or just beyond the universe. That is why one of the chief ways the early Christians chose to describe God was to say that God is 'infinite'.

Why must God be infinite?

When we say that God is infinite, we mean that God is not limited by anything else. There is nothing which sets limits to God and so makes God finite. God is not just one thing among other things of the same sort. But that means that we cannot think of God as a being, even as a very large being, who exists in addition to the universe – because if God were outside the universe, God would be limited by it and excluded from it. Theologians have sought many different ways of trying to express this point. Some have said that God is 'not a being, but Being-itself.' Some have said that God is 'the unlimited ocean of being.' Others have said that God is 'self-subsistent Being'. The common concern has been to deny that God is another thing, something like the things in the universe, but somehow bigger and better.

The idea that God is infinite is a very hard one to grasp, and perhaps the best most of us can do is to think in terms of some picture which may help us to think of it. As long as we remember that it is no more than a picture, which may be as misleading in its own way as Michelangelo's Old Man in the Sky, I would tentatively suggest the following way of thinking about God.

Instead of thinking of God as an invisible mind or person, somehow separate from us, try thinking of God as the one unlimited reality which includes us and the whole universe within itself. We are all finite and limited. But we are all parts of one reality which is unlimited and infinite; and that reality is 'God'. So I suggest that we might try thinking of God as the one unlimited reality of which all finite things – you, me, the trees, the stars, the galaxies – are parts.

Of course, I am not just saying that the universe *is* God, that God is nothing else but the physical universe. That would be quite wrong. If I said that, I would only be using the word 'God' to stand for what everybody else calls 'the universe'; and I do not mean that. But the universe can be seen as part of God. In the New Testament it is said that '*in him* we live and move and have our being' (Acts 17.28). Here is the idea that we are included in the infinite God.

If we say this, there is the danger that we might start thinking that, if we are 'part' of God, we are not free or responsible for our own actions; or that even evil things show what God is. To avoid this danger, we can use another picture and say that the physical universe is a collection of finite things which have their own proper natures, and many of these things have a real, though partial, freedom. God is completely different from anything in this universe, because God alone is unlimited and wholly self-determining. Nothing in the universe can ever be separated from God, and so everything is 'in him'; yet all finite things have their own proper being which makes them quite distinct from God. God has to be so unlike the universe, so unlike all finite, limited things that we cannot even imagine God properly. That is why, in the Old Testament, images of God were prohibited. Any image is bound to get God wrong; any image is bound to be finite.

All our words are about finite things. When we use a word for something, like a table or a chair, we use that word to pick out something which is different from other things, which marks out the limits of the thing, which refers to a finite reality. All our words have to do that; for they pick out slices of reality by marking off their limits from other things. So none of our words can apply properly to God. If God is infinite, and if all our words must apply to finite things, then none of our words are going to describe God properly. We cannot have words which are exact descriptions of God; nor can we have pictures which are exact representations of God.

I have said two main things. First, God has usually been thought by Christian theologians to be infinite, unlimited. This idea of infinity shows us two things about God. One is that God is not outside the universe, another finite being somewhere beyond the universe. God is not a tyrant God who keeps interfering with the universe from time to time, poking a finger in to keep the clockwork going or to put things right every now and again. God is not a finite being outside the universe; that is the first thing. So forget all those pictures of God as an old man with a beard.

Second, God, being infinite, cannot be exactly described by any human words or exactly pictured by any human images in any way. Even though God is not outside the universe, neither is God just the sum total of things in the universe. God is something which is completely indescribable. You could say – though it might be a little misleading – that God is the infinite source or origin of the universe. God is the infinite being which is expressed through the finite beings in the universe. The philosopher Plato once said, in what I think is a very beautiful phrase, 'Time is the moving image of eternity'. So we might say that the whole of space and time is the finite image of the infinite God. The whole of the universe expresses, in finite ways, a being which cannot itself be described.

So I am not saying that God is to be identified with the universe, with the finite things that we see around us. And I am not saying that God is another finite being outside the universe. I am saying that, if God is infinite, God cannot either be put 'into' the universe or put 'outside' it. What we have to say is that the universe may *express* this God in some way, though God cannot be *described* as a finite being at all.

How may we speak of God?

You may think that, even if it is true that God is infinite, there is nothing much that we can say of such a God.

How could we know what such a God is like? If, as I have said, none of our words can give an exact, correct description of God, so that we cannot say that God is thinking or feeling or desiring or willing, in the way that we think, feel or will; if all of these are only more or less inadequate pictures of God, does that mean that we cannot really say anything true about God at all? In one way it does. And that is a very important fact about God. Anything we say about God is only partially or inadequately true, in the sense we must mean it. All our words are inadequate to express the reality of God.

But sometimes we can convey important truths without being able exactly to describe them. The most obvious way in which this happens is in poetry. Paintings and music are important too, of course, but I want to consider poetry because poetry uses words. To most people, if they are prepared to make the effort, poetry can be so important that it transforms our whole view of life, our ways of feeling and knowing, our appreciation and perception of the things around us. It can convey things to us that could not be conveyed by a straightforward piece of prose.

Language about God is something like the language of poetry. When a poet writes a poem, he is trying to express something that he has seen about the world, some personal vision of the world. He is not trying to describe it in prose; that might be quite impossible. He is trying to evoke it, or convey it, or express it in a unique poetic way, through this particular use of language. The poetic use of language is not to increase your information about the world. We know facts about the world without having poetry. The use of words in poetry is to evoke in us a certain attitude or way of looking at things or feeling about things.

Of course, different poets have very different ways of looking at things. Some are very depressing or pessimistic; some are optimistic. Some are facile; some superficial. Some poets are very good; and others – most of them, I am afraid – are very bad. Not all poetry is religious, by any means; and not all poetry is good. But poetry is trying to convey something which cannot be conveyed simply by stating facts. It is trying to convey, let us say, a distinctive way of looking, that can only be understood and appreciated by learning to respond properly to poetry, by becoming at least imitative poets ourselves.

Now I think that language about God is very similar. It expresses a way of seeing, a certain attitude towards the world, a certain commitment and emotional response towards the world. Language about God can only be appreciated by our learning to take it on its own terms, by learning to experience for ourselves or at least to understand, the vision which it is conveying. So that reading language about God – and I do not mean dry academic theology, but the living language of worship and prayer – is conveying a distinctive approach to the world which we can learn to appreciate, by practice and sensitivity of approach. We may not appreciate it, just as we may not appreciate poetry. But it is possible to do so, and it may be important that we try.

If this is the use of religious language, what sort of view of the world is it trying to convey? I think we might say it is trying to convey that the world is the expression of a reality beyond it. I think that this is the reality which lies behind the picture of God being 'the maker of heaven and earth'. That picture almost irresistibly makes us think of the bearded muscle-man with his compasses, moulding the sky and the ground out of some sort of clay or primeval energy. But we know by now that we must discard such pictures once we have left the nursery school. What we have to say is that there is an infinite, literally indescribable reality which is the source and origin of all finite things, which expresses its character in and through them, and which is the true and enduring basis of whatever reality they have. To say that there is a 'maker of heaven and earth' is to say that the world of finite things is seen most truly when it is seen as the expression of a source and origin which is its essential truth and reality.

It is possible to look at the things in the world in many different ways. One way of looking at them for example, is the scientific way, as when you look at something and ask, 'How did it come to be the way it is?', 'Why is it as it is?', 'What laws does it obey?' and so on. That is one way of looking at the world. It is a dispassionate, analytical way which gives rise to science. Another way of looking at things is to see their beauty – not to ask how they came to be as they are, or what they are made of, but just to appreciate them, to regard them as beautiful in their own right. That more contemplative attitude is another distinct approach to the world. There is also an ethical or moral attitude. Then we do not just contemplate things, or ask how they arose. We ask rather what their needs are, how we can help them, or what they may claim from us. That is yet another attitude and is different from either the aesthetic attitude or the scientific attitude.

These are three sorts of attitudes we take to things in the world – the scientific, the artistic and the moral. The religious attitude is another, quite distinctive, sort of attitude. The religious attitude is one which sees the things of the world as pointing beyond themselves, as having a meaning which goes beyond their own reality. We are not asking the question, 'How does it come to be the way it is?' – the scientific question. We are not asking, 'How can I appreciate the beauty of this more fully?' – that is the aesthetic attitude. We are not asking, 'How can I help this being?' – that is the moral attitude. We are asking: 'What does this thing express about the nature of the underlying reality which gives it being and which keeps it in being? What is this saying about the fundamental nature of the world?' In the religious attitude, you might say that we are looking beyond the parts of the world to the whole, to see what lies behind and is expressed in things.

Of course, the religious attitude assumes that there is something which underlies the world which appears to us, that behind the finite realities in space and time there is an infinite reality which is appearing to us, which is 'revealing' itself to us in these finite things. The religious attitude is one which takes finite things as revelations of an infinite reality lying behind them, lying both in them yet also through them. 'Revelation' is the important word here. It literally means an unveiling, a drawing-apart of the veils of appearance to disclose the reality which underlies them. You can say that you have an experience of God when that revelation occurs, when the veils of the finite world are, as it were, drawn aside and you see the infinite reality which underlies them.

But you cannot describe that reality in prose. It needs the poetic approach, and it needs that direct personal experience of your own to see it; it has to happen to you, before you really appreciate it. But of course you can read about it happening, in the great religious works of the world. When you talk about 'revelations', you are really talking about these moments when people have seen the infinite expressed in certain finite things in the world.

There are two things to say about this. One is that different parts of the world obviously express the infinite in different ways. Some parts express its basic character better than others. The second thing to say is that some people are better at responding to revelations of God than others. Great transformations of religion happen when such individuals are able in some way to convey their very intense experiences of the infinite God to others. Religions are really traditions ultimately based on the revelations which certain inspired individuals have had, as God has been expressed to them in particular parts of the finite world. They have then expressed their experiences in poetic or symbolic forms, using ideas taken from their own cultures and societies to try to evoke an echo of their own apprehension in others. That is at least true in some way of most of the great religions that we now know in the world.

What we think the infinite is like will depend very much on the religious teacher whom we follow – the person who has had a particular experience and expressed it in a particular way – and it will depend upon the sort of context in which the experience occurred. If what I am saying is right, there will be no one final, exact, exhaustively correct description of God, because God is beyond all human concepts. The most that human concepts can do is to point, very inadequately, towards God. If we can remember that, it will be a great religious gain. For it will stop a lot of intolerance in our religious lives. Intolerance begins when people think that they have the one absolute final truth, and that people who disagree with them must be perverse or corrupt. It is very important to see that this is not necessarily so. No one has the absolute truth, and what evokes a vision of the infinite in one set of people at one time might very well fail to do so for another set of people. We are all in search of such visions of the infinite. We are not in the business of condemning others – or even ourselves – if, for one reason or another, we fail to have such a vision.

What I have tried to suggest is that, in thinking about God, we must first of all get rid completely of the idea of God as the old man in the sky, or as an invisible individual somewhere outside the physical universe. Instead, we should replace it with the idea of God as the infinite reality, which cannot be described exactly in any human words, which is expressed in all things in some way, which is in and yet beyond all finite things. This is, in fact, a perfectly traditional and orthodox Christian view, as expressed by all the earliest Christian theologians and as epitomized by that great scholar and saint, Thomas Aquinas. It has been something of a disaster that this doctrine of the infinity of God has evidently been forgotten, so that nowadays people seem to think that Christians mean by God some interfering old busybody who started the universe going and who sometimes comes back to fiddle around with it, but who on the whole lives on his own. The Christian religion, like most religions, is basically a search for God; and the search for God is the search for those finite expressions of the infinite reality which will be clearest and most fulfilling for us and for humanity as a whole.

Thus we are engaged on an unending exploration, which is guided by one who draws us onwards and encourages us always to move on towards greater visions yet to come.

2

How does the universe point to God?

If God is the source and origin of the finite world, can we say what this God is like? We have seen that God cannot really be described as God actually is. But we may be able to say something about God in relation to the world. Some ideas of how God is related to the world in which God expresses the divine nature may be more adequate than others. And one obvious way to discover what God is like is to look at the character of the finite world, to discover its most general nature, if we can, and to say what it is that this world expresses.

One of the features of the world which is clearest to us is that it is a world of rational order and law. In fact, the advance of the natural sciences, the existence and success of the natural sciences, is the best argument for the existence of God that there is. Some people think that science and religion are enemies. This is because there have been silly quarrels in the past between what some scientists have said and what some religious believers have said. We have all heard about the quarrels between Galileo and the Church, or between Huxley and

Bishop Wilberforce, who opposed the theory of evolution. These were quarrels between particular individuals, and they were quickly won by the scientists. But there is no quarrel, as such, between religion and the sciences.

Why science works

Indeed, it is no accident that science, in its modern sense, was born and grew up in a theistic, and in a specifically Christian, culture. Scientists like Isaac Newton, who were very concerned with belief in God, spent a lot of time in the study of the Bible as well as in making scientific discoveries. Newton said that when he was discovering the laws of nature, what he was really doing was reading the book of nature which God, the rational author of nature, had written. In other words, Newton was inspired to seek the laws of nature because he thought the world was created by a rational God. If you do not believe that God is rational – if you believe, for example, that there are lots of gods, with very arbitrary desires and wishes – then there is not much hope that science will be successful. Science did not get started in cultures where people thought that everything in the world was due to fate, blind chance or the unpredictable actions of many spirits and demi-gods. People began to think that science, in its modern sense, would be possible only when they began to think that there was a rational creator-God. For then we can believe that reason will be able to tell us the truth about the universe.

In this way, when people say that God exists, what they are saying is that the basis of the universe is rational.

Human reason at least gives us some clue to what it is really like, because it is itself founded on reason. Religion, far from being an irrational or anti-scientific thing, is the most rational activity that there is; and it is the foundation of the rational explanations of the world which science tries to provide.

It is worth thinking about the beginning of science in the Europe of the sixteenth and seventeenth centuries. Some people say that science began when people began to look at or observe the world around them more closely. This is not really true. People had been observing the world very carefully for hundreds, even thousands, of years already, and science had not begun. You could say that science really began, not when people began observing the world around them, but when they began to theorize about the world, when they began to ask themselves, not what the world looked like, but what a perfectly rational world would be like.

For example, Newton's 'First Law of Motion' states that an object, moving in a straight line at a certain speed, will keep going in the same direction and at the same speed unless something stops it. As far as observation goes, on earth, this is false. If you throw something away from you across a room, it will quite quickly fall to the floor. It will not carry on moving in a straight line for ever. If you relied just on observations, you would never decide that Newton's First Law was true. Now we have an explanation for why bodies drop to the floor. We know that it is because of the force of gravity, because of the pressure of air-particles, and so on. But that is a theory. To say that bodies move in a straight line unless they are stopped is simply a piece of abstract theory, unless you can test it in absolutely empty space. Newton, of course, was never able to visit a piece of empty space. So he was making a pure hypothesis or theory.

Science works in that way – not by observing, but by first of all inventing a rational theory and then by constructing experiments to test the theory, by controlling and not just by observing, nature. The fundamental presupposition, the basic starting-point, of all modern science, is that our rational theories about the world do fit the way the world is. A rational theory is one which, in mathematical terms, is simple and elegant. You seek for simplicity in a theory – that is, all the laws should be derivable from a few simple, general laws, and ideally from just one all-embracing law. And you seek also for elegance, or mathematical beauty, in a theory; in modern physics, some theories are held to be true almost entirely because they are elegant.

Many physicists believe that this whole complex universe only developed because there was a very precise balance of forces near its origin, the 'Big Bang'. For instance, very near the beginning of the universe, there was a ratio of precisely 1,000 photons to 1 nuclear particle. That ratio was necessary for the world to develop as it has done. There are a number of forces and elements that have to be exactly balanced in the same sort of way for this universe to give rise to conscious intelligent life. If things had been just a little different, stars and planets and rational beings would never have developed at all. This is an amazing fact that physicists have only recently discovered. But even this is unsatisfactory for a physicist like Steven Weinberg, for, he asks, why should that first state be the way it is? Why should it be just like that?

What can explain it? He says, as a physicist, 'We want a greater sense of logical inevitability.' Now those are his words. What he means by them is that the scientist would really like to explain absolutely everything, even why the very first state of the universe – if there was such a thing – was the way it was.

And this is the foundation of the scientific attitude – that you look for explanations for everything. You do not rest content with saying, 'Oh, it's just one of those odd things that happen around here'. You say: 'There must be a reason why it happens; there must be some explanation.'

Of course, as any philosopher will tell you, you cannot prove that everything must have a reason, that there must be a reason why everything happens. But unless you assume that everything has a reason, then you cannot do science. Even worse, you cannot live according to common sense, for even in common-sense, everyday life we assume that there has to be a reason for everything. When we get out of bed in the morning, we assume that if the floor were not there, there must be a good reason for this. Floors do not just disappear. Usually, the floor will be there. Why? Because the laws of nature usually do keep working; things do not just happen without any explanation. Floors do not simply disappear; my right leg is not in imminent danger of turning into a flowerpot. Camels do not suddenly materialize in the living-room. Things just do not happen without any explanation at all. In other words, we assume, both in common sense and in the sciences, that there must be a reason why things happen as they do. We may ask for the wrong sort of reason, or get the reason wrong; there does not always have to be the sort of reason we are looking for. But that there must be some adequate explanation, if only we could find it, is an axiom, a basic belief, without which ordinary life and science would not be possible.

God – the Ultimate Explanation

We can go further than this and say something about the sort of reason there must be. It must, in general, be a causal explanation. That is, there must be some law in accordance with which things happen. Law is a very rational thing; it is a sort of rule which physical objects seem to obey, always and everywhere. It is a rational principle, which stops things being haphazard or disorderly. It is true that, in physics, we often talk about chance. But we very rarely, and only with great restrictions, mean that things ever happen by pure chance. Nothing happens absolutely at random. Even if we do admit, in particle physics, what we call 'random events', these happen within very narrow boundaries of probability.

To put it in picture form, an electron, circling in orbit around an atomic nucleus, may suddenly jump from one orbit to another, and we might not be able to predict which one it is going to jump to. So we might call this a random factor in nature. But that randomness is very limited. We do not think, for example, that it could suddenly reverse its charge or turn into a minute goblin or disappear without trace. If such things happened, particle physics would become quite impossible, because we would never be able to repeat an experiment or predict what might happen next.

So events in the universe do have to happen in accordance with general laws. The philosopher Leibniz, who lived at about the same time as Isaac Newton, in the seventeenth century, said that nature is constructed in accordance with the simplest possible laws, which are so devised as to produce the richest and most complex set of effects. That is really the scientific ideal, one which appeals to the scientific mind, that from the simplest set of laws – ideally from one fundamental law of reality – there derives, by a natural process of development, the richest possible set of consequences.

A universe which was constructed like that would be the perfectly rational universe. Modern science assumes that the universe *is* like that, and modern science actually does work. That is the best argument for saying that the universe really is rational. It is intelligible. It is constructed in accordance with these general elegant principles that we should expect if it was a rational, explicable universe.

What this suggests then is that God, the basis and origin of this universe, is a rational consciousness. We are not trying to say that God has reason just like human reason. We are not trying to make God anthropomorphic, too much like human beings. But if you have a choice between saying that God is non-rational, or irrational or purely arbitrary, and that God is a rational being, ordering things in accordance with intelligible laws, then looking at the universe we are practically forced into saying that God is rational. We see that the basis of the universe is itself rational and intelligible; and that is why the human mind can investigate and explore the physical universe.

So belief in God is not some sort of purely irrational faith in the existence of something unknown. It is the belief that the universe has a rational cause; and *that* belief is just what the sciences need to confirm their faith that there are universal and rational laws of nature. It is a belief which has been presented in traditional Christian theology by talking about 'proofs of God'. But we must be careful not to misunderstand the word 'proof'.

Nowadays, influenced by mathematics, we think of a proof as something which is absolutely convincing. If somebody comes up with a proof in mathematics – for example, that 2 + 2 = 4 – then you are either ignorant or you are lying if you say you do not believe it. There cannot be rational disagreement about a proof. So some people think that proofs of God should be convincing in just the same way – if they work and you do not accept them, then you must be either ignorant or immoral. But we know that many very intelligent people know all about the proofs of God, and still do not believe in God. So how can they be proofs?

The fact is that they are not infallible proofs at all, and they were never meant to be. What they do is set out what the world must ultimately be like, if it really is, as both the scientists and common sense seem to assume, based on absolutely rational laws, if it is completely explicable. We can never prove that the world can be completely explained; that must be a sort of faith. All we can say is that it is a faith that modern science is based on, and which seems to be justified by the sheer amazing success of science. Now, if the world is totally explicable, the first and most famous proof – the causal argument – sets out to show that there must be a being of a certain sort, with a certain character; and this, it says, is 'God'.

The argument starts out by saying that we do, or at least we should, always look for an explanation of every event. So we must assume that there is a cause – an explanation – for everything that happens, if only we look hard enough. That is the basis of the scientific attitude. I do not see any reason why we should arbitrarily give it up at some point and say: 'That is enough: I am not going to look for any more reasons. I will just accept what there is from now on.' That is the starting-point, then – there must be an explanation for everything.

Next, the argument goes on to point out that these explanations cannot go on for ever. We cannot go on for ever saying that everything must be explained by something else. For then there would never be a complete explanation at all. Wherever you got to, there would always be something left unexplained. Now, again, nobody can absolutely prove that there must be a complete explanation. The point is that it is our intellectual curiosity which drives us to ask for a complete explanation, which leads us to keep on asking 'Why?' until we get a finally satisfying answer. That answer will never come if explanations go on for ever. So let us suppose that they do not go on for ever, that there really is a complete explanation, which will answer all our questions. What would it be like?

It is obvious, when you think about it, that if the world is going to be really intelligible, fully rational, there will have to exist something which not only explains other things, but also explains itself as well. It is impossible to give a good example of such a thing; because, says the believer in God, there only is, and only ever could be, one such thing, and that is God. But I will suggest a rough analogy. Suppose I tell you that I want to cross the road. You ask me why, and I say, 'Because I want to get to the other side'. Not totally satisfied, you ask me why again, and I say, 'Because I want an ice-cream'. Feeling awkward, you go on asking why. 'Well,' I reply, 'because I like ice-cream'. If you continue to ask why, I will probably be stumped for an answer. I just like it; that is an ultimate fact about me and ice-cream. Now this is not self-explanatory, because I cannot explain why I like ice-cream. It is something I can give you no further reason for; it is the end of one chain of reasons. It explains my conduct, sometimes. But I cannot explain it.

Now the example is not very good, because my taste could be explained physiologically, no doubt, and because it is hardly self-explanatory. I have only suggested it to give some idea of what the end of a chain of reasons might look like. What we want, in the case of the universe, however, is an end to the chain of reasons which really is not explicable by anything other than itself, but which does explain its own nature and existence completely. If there is a complete explanation of the universe, there must be a being – God – which nothing else could ever explain, but which fully explains itself. God must be self-explanatory. Can we imagine that? The plain fact is that we cannot. We cannot imagine any being which would be truly self-explanatory. We cannot imagine God. But that is just what theologians have always said. What we can do, however – and what we have just done, in fact – is to say what a self-explanatory being would have to be, and to say that there must be one, if the universe is to be completely explicable.

God has to be a totally unique sort of being, so that, if we could fully understand God, we would say: 'Now I understand why God is the sort of being God is. I see that God could not be any other way than God is. I see that there is really no alternative to God. God just has to exist.' We can only have a hint, a glimpse, of what such a being might be like. It is beyond our understanding. So there is always the possibility that the very idea is illusory or impossible. I do not at all want to argue God into existence, just by some abstract argument in a book. If I ask what is really going on in arguments, or proofs, like this, I think the truth is as follows:

We begin by looking at the universe, as scientists see it. It seems to show an amazingly elegant and rational structure; it seems to provide just the sorts of rational explanation that the human mind, when it is properly trained, looks for. Now we think of extending this process of investigation and explanation as far as possible, and we arrive at the idea of a complete explanation, which would make the universe totally rational.

Now this idea is so far from our human experience that we are not really sure, any longer, whether it really does make sense, whether there could be such a thing. But we see the idea of it – the idea of God – as a sort of ultimate goal of rational understanding, a reality distinct in kind from anything we come across in the finite world, but a self-sufficient reality upon which everything else might depend for its existence. This argument for God, therefore, points us in a certain direction – in the direction of greater and greater understanding. But it points to something beyond our experience, an idea which we cannot really grasp. And this is just where the argument becomes more than merely abstract (like some purely academic exercise), because it is in fact an exercise in the training of vision, in pointing our minds towards a reality just 'beyond' our understanding but in the direction of greater, not less, understanding.

Its real aim is to evoke in us a sort of vision – a sense of the world as a set of fleeting, changing, always dying instants which at every moment depends upon and expresses an unchanging, stable and somehow complete and fully rational order of being. One reason the proofs of God are not like mathematical proofs is that they do depend, in the end, upon evoking this vision of the unlimited; and no purely rational process can do that.

God – the Ultimate Cause

So we get the idea of God as the 'First Cause of all things'. God is not that which comes first in time, as though God was just the first of a series of similar things. In fact it is obvious, when you think about it, that, if God is the origin of the whole universe, God must be the cause of space and time as well. Therefore God must be beyond space and time as we know it. God cannot be just the first thing in time; God must be the creator and explanation of time – God must be eternal. When we say that God is the cause of the universe, we do not mean that God came at the beginning and started the whole process going. We mean that God is beyond time. Time and space and everything in them all depend upon God; they could not exist without God. God alone is self-existent – God can exist without depending upon anything else, and needs nothing else in order to exist.

If God is beyond time, it follows that God must also be beyond change, as we know it. For all changes take place in time. So we talk of God as unchanging, or immutable; 'Change and decay in all around we see; O Thou who changest not, abide with me.' The changeless and self-existent God, eternal and without end or beginning – that is the God which we might dimly apprehend as underlying and sustaining all the changing, dependent and dying things of this visible universe. And it is the being which, so far as we can see, is required if the scientist's faith in the rationality of the universe is finally to be justified.

So we can see how science and religion meet in this idea of an eternal, unchanging, self-existent source of all things. But there is one problem which may seem difficult. I have said that God is indescribable by human beings. But I have also said that God is totally comprehensible. How can I say both these things at once? The solution is to distinguish the divine nature as it really is from what we can understand of God. Human beings cannot hope to comprehend God, simply because our intellects are so limited. But the divine nature in itself is wholly comprehensible. There is, in other words, a complete explanation; the universe is fully rational. But though we can know or believe that, we cannot work it all out. The ideal of a complete explanation remains for us an ever-receding goal, which we will never reach, because our minds are incapable of grasping it as a whole. The reality of God blinds us, it has been said, not by its obscurity, but by excess of light.

So we have very little positive idea of what God is like. We have no private window into the inner life of God. Our descriptions of God are all in negative terms: that God is *not* in time; that God is *not* brought into existence by anything else; that God does *not* depend on anything else; that God is *not* changed by anything else. If we speak of God as a rational consciousness, that is just because, however inadequate it is, it is the best model we have for a basis for the universe which makes it explicable and intelligible. It is less misleading than saying that God is an irrational and arbitrary unconscious power. In other words, the origin of the world is more, and not less, than human reason and consciousness.

So what I have tried to suggest is that belief in God, as the eternal and self-existent one, is a further spelling-out of the nature of the infinite being which is expressed in the finite world. As we look at the world, with its rational, ordered, mathematical elegance, it seems entirely reasonable to think that its basis lies in a rational, self-existent consciousness. That is what most Christians believe. They do not believe in that old anthropomorphic God whose creation of the world consisted in giving it a push in the beginning and then dozing off for aeons of masterly inactivity. When we say that God is the 'Father almighty, maker of heaven and earth', we are saying that God is the eternal consciousness which gives rise to and expresses itself in the universe of general, intelligible law which science investigates.

God is the Father, as the ultimate source of all things. God is almighty, because God brings all things into being and explains what and why they are. God determines what they shall be; and, as the ultimate cause, God cannot be changed or modified or obstructed in any way that God does not himself decree. God's power over everything in the world is unlimited; and God's wisdom, as shown in the things God has made, is breath-taking. We begin to see where worship starts when we realize the unlimited power and wisdom of the eternal God. And that realization dawns as the sciences discover more and more of the beauty, the vastness and the rational structure of the universe within which we exist.

3

Does God have a purpose?

We have seen that when Christians speak of God as 'the Father almighty, maker of heaven and earth', this is picture language which can be conveyed to the youngest or simplest minds. But it also has a much more subtle and profound meaning, which is that the infinite, unlimited reality expressed in our finite universe is an eternal and self-existent being, the source of all other things and unlimited in power and wisdom. It is the source of the rational and ordered laws upon which our universe is founded. So it is right to think of God as that rational consciousness which is the origin and basis of nature. It is right to think of this God with reverence and awe, as being unlimited in power and wisdom.

The argument I have set out here was not, of course, used in that form in the Bible. Nevertheless, those who reflected about God and who wrote about God in the scriptures undoubtedly did see the world of nature as the expression of just such a God of power and wisdom. They did not have the modern scientific world-view. They had not worked out all the implications of the world being the creation of a rational consciousness. But they could see that nature showed the existence and influence of a being of great power and wisdom. They could say: 'The heavens declare the glory of God, and the firmament showeth his handiwork.' They saw that the world depended upon an underlying power for its existence; and they could see something of that power in the events of their daily lives.

It does not take a sophisticated argument to show that God is the creator of heaven and earth. Just the direct and natural perception by the human mind of the beauty and order of things can see the presence and power and wisdom of God continually expressed in the things and happenings of the world. That is an important part of believing in God. But we need also to go on and ask, 'Is there any purpose in this world?' There is design and order; the origin of the world does appear to have unlimited power. But is there any reason why the being of God should be expressed in this way at all? Again, it is natural for us to think that there is a purpose. But may we not be simply deluding ourselves?

Why are we here?

Many people have thought that human beings are such very small parts of the universe and human minds so very limited, that any attempt by us to say what the purpose of the whole of the universe might be is unduly arrogant and quite fruitless. We live on a small planet of a small star on the fringe of one of many galaxies. How can such a minute part of the universe make any guess at all about the purpose of the whole thing? Why, indeed, should we think that there is any purpose?

One reason for thinking that there is a purpose is that, once we have said that the universe expresses a rational consciousness, it is very natural to think that the existence of this universe has some purpose, that the consciousness expresses itself for some reason. In fact, we have already said that the scientific attitude is one that always asks for the reason why things exist. Although, in the sciences, asking for a reason is usually asking for the cause – for what brought things into existence – it may well be that in the end the only satisfactory reason why the universe exists needs to be given in terms of a purpose. We might want to say, not only how the universe began, but what it is aimed at, what is its goal, what it is directed towards. We have to ask: 'Does it look as though there is any purpose for which this universe could have been created?' That is a natural and proper question, one that follows from the scientific frame of mind.

Is it reasonable, then, to think that our universe has a purpose? When the Bible was written, people had a very different view of what the universe was like. They thought that the universe was a fairly small place and that the earth was in the centre of it. The earth was a sort of flat dish, and the heavens were placed over it like a dome, with the stars, the sun and the moon hung on that dome like lamps. Human beings had existed for only about 2,000 years and were the centre of God's attention. It should be remembered, of course, that people then also believed in a whole host of 'heavenly beings' – angels, archangels and so on – which existed beyond the heaven and the earth, so the whole universe was not quite as small as this picture suggests. There were hosts of heavenly beings, with which God was also concerned. Nevertheless, as far as this universe went, the scale of things was much smaller than we now think of it, and human beings were much nearer the centre of it. So when people asked about the purpose of God then, they were simply asking about life on the planet earth.

We cannot now look at things in that way. We know that human beings are on the periphery of the universe, that we are very unlikely to be the centre of God's purposes in the whole of creation. The earth is not even the centre of the solar system, let alone the centre of the universe. Does this mean that we cannot talk any longer about the purpose of God? Not at all. However vast or beautiful or awe-inspiring the universe is, most of it consists of empty space and lifeless rocks, roaring suns and clouds of gas. However wonderful we think these are, there is a sense in which the smallest and most insignificant conscious being is more valuable than all those millions and millions of light-years of empty space. Size is not everything; and the largest and most beautiful thing there is, if it is not perceived by anyone, not appreciated and valued by anyone, is totally without value. Things only have value when they are perceived by someone. For to say that a thing has value is to say that it is worth choosing, and things are only worth choosing for the effect they have on some consciousness or other. So an unconscious universe is a universe without value.

Universal values?

We see that there are lots of things which may be of value to us. The most obvious one is happiness. We value happiness; we think it is worth choosing; we seek it when we do not have it and rest content when we do. Happiness is something which is intrinsically good; it is good for its own sake; it is something that we would choose for its own sake. So, strange as it may seem at first, it is true that even the happiness of one lowly animal on a small planet is of more value than the whole of the rest of the universe, if there is no consciousness anywhere in it. For nothing is of value unless it is experienced by some conscious being, who would choose it for its own sake.

Now what sorts of things are really worth while, worth choosing for their own sakes? There may be many such things; they are often lumped together under the general term 'happiness'. That can cover a host of different things, from digging the garden to listening to a symphony, climbing a mountain or talking with friends. In fact, it can cover so many different things that it may be a rather misleading term, making us think that only one thing is worth while, when there are many worthwhile things all the time. I suspect that it is just not possible to make a complete list of all the worthwhile things, the good things that exist. But what we can do is to pick out some general sorts of things which are of value, which are intrinsically good.

First, we might think of knowledge – not just the bare knowing of a lot of facts, but experience and awareness of people and places, the growing understanding of what they are like, and the sense of familiarity and enjoyment that we have in knowing them. That sort of knowledge which grows towards a sensitive understanding and real appreciation of things, in their particularity, is surely a very great good. The philosopher Aristotle thought that it was the greatest of all goods, including both the appreciation of beauty and the understanding of the reasons of things. Maybe that would be a little too refined or intellectual for most of us, but we cannot deny that such knowledge is an intrinsic good – it is one of the things worth choosing for its own sake.

Another thing that is intrinsically good is creative activity. I do not mean anything particularly grand by this, but just the making of things which can express our own skill and individuality. At its best, of course, people produce great works of art. But everyone can do something creative, and the exercise of skill and ability to produce something which we have made is also worth while for its own sake. To be self-determining, free and able to do whatever one chooses; to have plans and projects which one can put into action; to be able to shape one's own future and the world in which one lives – these are goods which any rational being would choose, if it could.

Yet another good which appeals to most people, and perhaps the deepest of all, is love. I do not mean the romantic feeling of being 'in love', though that is no doubt very exciting. And I do not mean the emotionless doing good to others, without being involved with them in any way. I really mean that sort of involvement with the lives of others which makes us grieve with them in their sorrow and rejoice in their happiness, which gives us a care and concern for their individual development, and which gives us a delight in being with them as well as an obligation to help them in trouble. There is perhaps no greater good than mutal co-operation between friends; and if we are lucky enough to have such a relationship with anyone, we will undoubtedly feel this to be the most meaningful and profound of human experiences.

If we think about the things that are most meaningful to us – which give us a sense of worthwhileness and value, and which we would really choose just for their own sakes – I think that they would almost certainly fall under one of these four headings – happiness, knowledge, creative freedom and love. These are the things which make human life worthwhile, which make us really more human and fulfilled. You may well want to add 'virtue' to this list – the human capacity, which animals do not seem to have, to do what is right for its own sake, in the face of temptation or difficulty. I am sure that morality is one of the distinctive features of human life, and that it is in learning to live morally that people become most truly human. We should be just, truthful and loyal, whatever the cost to us personally. But if you think about it, morality seems to be the pursuit of happiness, knowledge and creative freedom for all who are capable of them. Justice is concerned with making such goals available to everyone, and with the impartial distribution of advantages and disadvantages. Honesty is necessary to the growth of knowledge. And loyalty is part of the pattern of love. So virtue is precisely the free pursuit of the four worthwhile goals of human life, just for their own sake, without regard to personal benefit. We are to pursue whatever makes for an increase in happiness, in knowledge, in creative freedom and in love between people. That is our purpose, simply because, when we sit down to reflect, we see that these goals really are worth while; they are what we may call 'intrinsic values' – things worth choosing for their own sake.

Now when we say that they are worth while, we do not just mean that people like choosing them. We mean that they are *worth* choosing, they have a value of their own, even if some people cannot be bothered to pursue them. Any being at all – not just a human being, but an extra-terrestrial or a supernatural being too – would find them worth choosing. The point about humans is that they can freely choose them, even when it is difficult to do so and when there are lots of temptations not to do so. We have moral freedom; and that means that we do not have to choose them. We can choose misery, ignorance, laziness and selfishness, if we want to. In fact, most people do, to some extent; that is largely what Christians mean by saying that the world is 'in sin' – people fail to choose what is truly worth while.

We can easily understand that somebody may just not want to be bothered to learn more or that they would prefer to enjoy themselves passively, by being entertained rather than getting up and doing something creative and helpful to others. All the same, we know perfectly well that happiness, knowledge, creativity and love are worth while. Just ask yourself these questions. Is it better to be happy or sad? Is it better to have knowledge or to be ignorant? Is it better to be free or to be a slave? Is it better for people to help one another or to ignore each other? We will have to admit that happiness, knowledge, freedom and love are obviously better. The reason we may not choose them in particular cases is that they are too much trouble, or that what is in theory better may actually be too costly to us, personally, at the moment. 'Ignorance is bliss,' we may say. Or: 'At least, as a slave, I do not have to make hard decisions.' Or: 'I prefer to keep myself to myself.' Human beings will understand that only too well.

But the question we are concerned with at the moment is not: 'Why should I be moral?' It is this: 'Suppose you are wondering whether the universe has a purpose. To answer that question, you will have to ask whether there are worthwhile states towards which it is moving. And to answer that, you will first of all have to decide whether there are any really worthwhile states, and what they would be. So, are there any states which are worth while for their own sake, and which are clearly and unquestionably goals worth aiming at?' I suggest that, upon reflection, we must all agree that there are such states, that a community of beings which realized happiness, knowledge, creative freedom and love, would be one which realized these states. Such beings might not be human. They could have any shape or form at all. But we would still know that their form of life was a worthwhile one. We would admire it and would surely wish that, if it were not so difficult, we could have such a life too.

So it is not just anthropomorphic prejudice; it is not just silly arrogance, which makes us think that in human life there is a value that is intrinsically worth while. The fact is that the development and existence of conscious beings which can grow in knowledge, creativity, love and happiness is something which is worth having; it is what I have called an 'intrinsic value'. It does not matter what those beings look like, or what form their society may take; they might be the strangest space-monsters imaginable. But if they can aim at those sorts of values, then they share something very important with human life. Now, once we have seen that there are some things which are worth while for their own sake, we can go further and ask whether the universe looks as if it is directed towards the existence of such things.

We call a process 'purposive' when we can explain it best as directed towards a goal which is of value. If a process does not issue in anything valuable, or if it is not directed towards the realization of that value, then we would not call it purposive. So the universe can be seen as purposive if it seems to be a process which is directed towards realizing values. And this means that the laws of the universe must be directed towards the existence of conscious, free and rational beings which can choose to realize intrinsic values.

A value, of course, does not have to be something static, as though it has to be just the last state of a process. The process itself may be of value. For example, if we take a simple human activity like mountain-climbing, the value of this activity does not lie simply in its last state, in standing on top of the mountain. If it did, we could achieve it much more easily by taking a helicopter straight to the top of the mountain. But this would seem to miss the point. It is the activity of climbing which is valued. So processes, or activities, can be of value as well. Thus the activity of rational beings in realizing value may itself be a great value. Such activity, carried out in the face of temptation or opposition, is what we call 'virtue'. A purposive universe will be one which issues in the existence of conscious beings finding happiness in the free pursuit of virtue.

When you think of it like that, it is no longer absurd to say that human existence might be at least part of the purpose of the universe. Our physical smallness is really beside the point. If the universe has a purpose, then it lies in the existence of a consciousness which achieves happiness through its own activity. This, it seems, is just what human life, in this universe, is like. The whole process of the evolution of the universe has led to the existence of human societies in which it is possible to find happiness in the development of knowledge, creativity and friendship. In this way it is very plausible to see the universe as expressing purpose.

The goal of evolution

Some people say that modern science has shown that there are no purposes in the universe, that everything happens by blind necessity or pure chance. That is very far from being true. Indeed it is precisely the theory of evolution – one of the most far-reaching insights of modern science – which gives us the clearest and deepest insight into what it means for the universe to be purposive. When we think of evolution, what we think about is a development from a few simple elements – a few simple particles and the laws governing their interaction – by processes of natural change to a situation, first of all of organic, self-sustaining life, and eventually of that sort of self-directing conscious life that we find in human beings. That evolution, that development of new qualities which had not previously existed in the universe, does seem to show a purposive direction. Indeed, it is very hard to see the development of conscious life by such natural processes as anything other than purposive.

This is not the sort of purpose that is imposed on the universe from outside, as though an external God had to keep interfering to cause certain things which were not natural to the universe itself. It is the universe itself, in its own structure, which is inherently purposive; it seems to be aimed towards this goal of consciousness and value. The purpose is the inner direction of evolution itself, present from the first moment of its existence and gradually unfolding through time to produce new, more complex and valuable properties.

It is true that some evolutionary biologists think of animal evolution as non-purposive, as happening by random mutation, because of which, by chance, some specimens survived better than others. But the theory itself can never establish that there is no purpose in the process. There may be more than randomness in the sorts of mutation which happen; it may be more than mere chance that certain species survive and others do not. In other words, there may well be a guiding, directing influence in the process, even though we cannot pick out exactly where it works, or prove beyond any doubt that it is present. What we have to do is look at the whole process – and at the evolution of the earth from the first state of the universe as well as animal evolution on the earth – and ask whether it looks more random or more purposive. What I have suggested is that, while there is no conclusive proof either way, what has happened is just what one would expect from a purposive process; it would be very strange if a random process had copied the purposive in such an exact way purely by chance.

The evolutionary perspective, which gives us an overall view of the whole universe as an evolving, developing system, is one of the greatest changes in our view of the world which modern science has brought about. No biblical writer could have thought of it. At the time of Jesus, they were really expecting the world to end at any moment and God's purpose to be suddenly brought about by a miraculous intervention. They could not think of any other way in which it could happen. Now we have a perspective of thousands, even millions of years, ahead of us; and we can see God's kingdom as the final goal of evolution, the achieved society of growing love, knowledge, creative cooperation and friendship. We have to give up, as pre-scientific, the picture of humanity created perfect in the Garden of Eden just a few thousand years ago, of a sudden fall into sin and of an equally sudden end to this wicked world just around the corner. In its place, we must adopt the scientific picture of a long, slow development of rational conscious life from inorganic matter by natural processes, of humanity as evolving and surviving by lust and aggression as well as by love and friendship, and of further, future progress for the human race towards the goal set by God, the realization of goodness by the free activities of his creatures.

The adoption of this evolutionary picture gives new life and sense to the idea of God's purpose. We can see it now as the direction immanent in the world-process itself, the goal-orientated process of evolution in which we are called to take a responsible part. God's purpose is not a plan arbitrarily imposed on the world by some external being; it is the inner direction and goal of the world itself.

There are many more things that could be said about God, and philosophers and theologians throughout the ages have developed the idea of God in many different and complicated ways. I have just tried to sketch a basic idea of God which is very widely accepted in many traditions. I have concentrated on God as the ultimate rational explanation of the universe, and as a reality which gives a moral goal to the existence of the universe and of human beings. In the end, however, what matters most is the personal experience millions of people have of an infinite and eternal reality which is known and felt in and through many finite things and events. William Blake put it very well:

> To see a world in a grain of sand
> And a heaven in a wild flower,
> Hold infinity in the palm of your hand
> And eternity in an hour.

To find those words meaningful is to begin to understand what we mean by 'God'.

Further reading

Here is a short list of books that can guide you further in your exploration of the topics discussed in the preceding pages. All are available through bookshops, or direct from the publisher at <www.spckpublishing.co.uk>.

Craig Hovey, *What Makes Us Moral?* (2012)
Alister McGrath, *The Dawkins Delusion?* (2007)
Alister McGrath, *Why God Won't Go Away* (2011)
John Polkinghorne, *Reason and Reality* (SPCK Classics, 2011)
John Polkinghorne, *Science and Religion in Quest of Truth* (2011)
Keith Ward, *Christianity: A guide for the perplexed* (2007)
Keith Ward, *The Word of God?* (2010)